make it in
Minutes

Mini-Boxes

make it in
Minutes

Mini-Boxes

MARIAN BALLOG

LARK BOOKS

A Division of Sterling Publishing Co., Inc., New York

Book Editor
Catherine Risling

Copy Editor
Erika Kotite

Photographer
Zachary Williams
Williams Visual
Ogden, UT

Stylist
Annie Hampton

Book Designer
Kehoe + Kehoe Design
Associates, Inc.
Burlington, VT

*Other Books
in this Series:*

Make It in Minutes:
Greeting Cards

Make It in Minutes:
Mini-Books

Make It in Minutes:
Beaded Jewelry

Make It in Minutes:
Party Favors
& Hostess Gifts

A Red Lips 4 Courage Communications, Inc., book
www.redlips4courage.com
Eileen Cannon Paulin
President
Catherine Risling
Director of Editorial

Library of Congress Cataloging-in-Publication Data

Ballog, Marian, 1953-
   Mini-boxes / Marian Ballog. -- 1st ed.
      p. cm. -- (Make it in minutes)
   Includes index.
   ISBN 1-60059-090-X (hardcover)
   1. Box craft. 2. Box making. I. Title.
   TT870.5.B35 2007
   745.593--dc22
                                    2006036802

10 9 8 7 6 5 4 3 2 1

First Edition

Published by Lark Books, A Division of
Sterling Publishing Co., Inc.
387 Park Avenue South, New York, N.Y. 10016

Text © 2007, Marian Ballog
Photography © 2007, Lark Books
Illustrations © 2007, Lark Books

Distributed in Canada by Sterling Publishing,
c/o Canadian Manda Group, 165 Dufferin Street
Toronto, Ontario, Canada M6K 3H6

Distributed in the United Kingdom by GMC Distribution Services,
Castle Place, 166 High Street, Lewes, East Sussex, England BN7 1XU

Distributed in Australia by Capricorn Link (Australia) Pty Ltd.,
P.O. Box 704, Windsor, NSW 2756 Australia

If you have questions or comments about this book, please contact:
Lark Books
67 Broadway
Asheville, NC 28801
(828) 253-0467
Manufactured in China
All rights reserved

ISBN 13: 978-1-60059-090-0
ISBN 10: 1-60059-090-X

For information about custom editions, special sales, premium and corporate
purchases, please contact Sterling Special Sales Department at (800) 805-5489
or specialsales@sterlingpub.com.

"A box without hinges, key, or lid,
yet golden treasure inside is hid."

—J.R.R. Tolkien

Introduction

Miniature boxes are little treasures that appeal to all ages. They send good wishes for birthdays and weddings and celebrate favorite things, from shell collections to restaurants and family pets. They note happy times like road trips, gardening in springtime, and children's sports. Hopes and dreams, special times, and peaceful moments can all be captured in something as simple as a little box dressed with readily available ribbons, bits of trim, glitter, and charms.

Fun and practical are not forgotten, either. Mini-boxes are specially designed to hold everyday items. House keys, credit cards, and sewing needles and thread find tiny homes created just for them.

Before you discard an empty container, think of the possibilities. Mint tins, adhesive bandage boxes, and even dental floss boxes are all great recyclable sources for the projects featured throughout this book.

Mini-boxes are not only fun to create; they are quick and easy craft projects you can make in minutes.

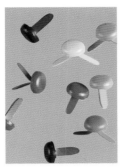
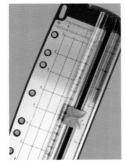

CHAPTER 1

At first you might not really notice them—small boxes, often with very different original purposes. These boxes draw us in to their little decorated world. Mini-boxes are readily available at craft stores and jewelry counters. They can even be found in the candy section of your local convenience store. They come in tin, wood with tiny hinges and clasps, and paper or cardboard shaped like ovals, circles, squares, hearts, and even shopping bags. Before you know what has hit you, you might find yourself squinting at a grocery store shelf, trying to decide which shape of mint tin to purchase for the next project you want to make from these pages. Even the enthusiastic recycler will be happy—most of the projects are made from discarded tins and dispensers.

Embellishments

Acrylic paint

Paints are sold in a variety of colors, finishes, and thicknesses. Dimensional acrylic paint comes in a tube with decorating tips, much like cake frosting, and can be built up in thick layers.

Beads

Large and small beads can be used on mini-boxes as feet to elevate the box or as surface decoration. Micro beads can be applied to word cut-outs to add texture. Adhere larger beads with strong-hold glue, glue dots, or double-sided tape. Smaller beads can be adhered with craft glue or double-sided tape.

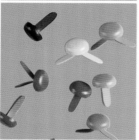

Brads

A common office product and now a popular paper crafting essential, brads come in geometric and novelty shapes in a wide variety of colors and metallic finishes. Place brad through a pierced or punched hole and open the prongs on the back. Trim extra length of prongs if necessary so they don't show from the front.

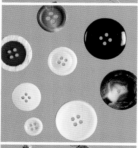

Buttons

Buttons have come a long way from the basic round shape. They are available at craft and fabric stores in themed novelty sets and large-quantity assortment bags. Adhere with glue dots, hot glue, strong-hold glue, or craft glue.

Charms

Metal and resin charms are found in jewelry-making and bead shops and craft stores. Adhere with glue dots, foam dots, strong-hold glue, or a hot glue gun.

Glitter

Glitter is available in a rainbow of colors with sheer and opaque qualities. Textures range from ultra fine to chunky grains to snowflake-like drifts of mica. A solid bond is ensured by using double-sided tape, glitter glue, or adhesive paper. A fine tip for glitter glue is essential for detailed work.

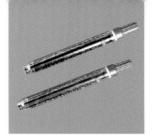

Leafing pens

Leafing pens are metal-barreled pens that dispense paint, rather than ink, through a felt tip. Metallic gold, silver, and copper leafing pens can be used to cover writing and bridge the gaps between tin boxes and paper elements.

Paper

In addition to cardstock and decorative paper, bits of paper from everyday life can be used to embellish mini-boxes. Stamps, postcards, family photos, toy currency, and ticket stubs can all decorate mini-boxes. To preserve the originals or to reduce the image size, simply photocopy the paper element. Adhere with acid-free adhesive, double-sided tape, glue dots, or foam dots.

Ribbons and trims

Ribbon, twill tape, and beaded trims should be selected with an eye to their widths so that sides and border edges of tins and boxes are evenly covered. Consider luxurious textures and intricate weaves for formal looks. Also consider string, twine, measuring tapes, rickrack, and lace, both new and vintage.

Rub-ons

Adhesive decals of alphabets, sewing stitches, and many other fun designs are applied to flat surfaces using a craft stick. Personalize a tag, miniature file folder, ribbon, or twill tape with a personal message or monogram.

Silk and paper flowers

Available in a wide variety of colors and sizes, silk flowers can be adhered to mini-boxes with a hot glue gun, foam tape, glue dots, or craft glue. Adhere center embellishments with glue dots or a hot glue gun.

Stickers

Alphabet stickers and other self-adhesive paper designs in many styles, fonts, colors, and themes are useful for creating a theme or adding journaling, titles, monograms, and dates. Words and phrases come in paper and epoxy forms of sticker embellishments.

Adhesives

Acid-free adhesive dispenser
Acid-free adhesive dispensers contain a dry form of glue dispensed in a small dot or linear form. It can turn corners and bond papers with little or no puckering. In certain uses, it can bond non-paper items like thin ribbon with paper.

Craft glue
Craft glue refers to clear-drying white glue somewhat thicker than the classroom white glue. Read the label to ensure that the glue is intended for paper, fabric, or metal.

Double-sided tape
Double-sided tape comes in various widths and is an important ingredient in many of the projects featured throughout this book. With the backing left on, it can be cut or punched into decorative shapes and used to adhere glitter, seed beads, or micro beads to projects.

Foam dots
Foam dots are useful when applying a decorative element that needs a little "lift" or elevation. Foam is sandwiched between two sticky surfaces and can be cut to fit. Save your craft scissors by cutting foam dots with the paper backing left on to shield the adhesive.

Foam tape
Foam is layered between two adhesive strips sold on a roll or in cut pieces readily available at scrapbooking and craft stores.

Glitter glue
Glitter adhesive is listed for all projects using glitter and has a thicker consistency than many craft glues.

time-saving tip
Double-Duty Paper
If you don't have double-sided paper for a project or can't find the right combination of prints, simply make your own by adhering two coordinating pieces together using an adhesive application machine.

Glue dots

Glue dots are thin or thick spots of glue on a sticker-release paper. They can be applied directly to a surface, such as paper, or rolled and cut for adhering tiny charms or frames.

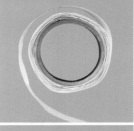

Glue stick

This solid form of glue is commonly available and used in a few of the projects featured throughout this book. Keep a container of wet hand wipes nearby to keep hands free of excess glue that might transfer to a project.

Hot glue sticks

Glue sticks are commonly available and used in conjunction with a hot glue gun for adhering heavier embellishments. Either hot melt or cool melt glue sticks will work.

Strong-hold glue

Strong-hold glue is sold in a squeeze tube and bonds a wide variety of surfaces including glass, metal, and plastic. Useful for attaching glass or plastic beads to metal and wood boxes as feet.

Vellum adhesive

Vellum adhesive appears invisible or nearly invisible behind vellum paper. Other ways to adhere vellum are to use glue dots and then hide them with buttons, flowers, etc.

Additional Supplies

There are many everyday items that will help you craft and embellish miniature boxes, including:

- Computer and printer
- Cosmetic sponges
- Cotton swabs
- Craft scissors
- Paper plate
- Paper towels
- Pencils
- Plastic cup
- Plastic knife
- Ruler
- Sandpaper
- Toothpicks

Tools

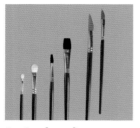

Artist brushes

Bone folder

Colored pencils

Craft knife

Cutting mat

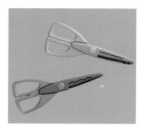

Decorative-edge scissors

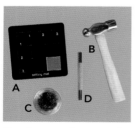

Eyelet-setting tools
A Setting mat   C Eyelets
B Craft hammer   D Eyelet setter

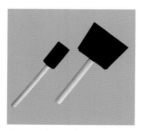

Foam brushes

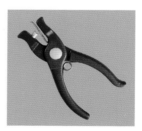

Hole punch

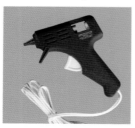

Hot glue gun

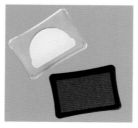

Inkpad

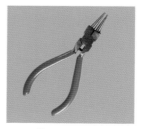

Needle-nose pliers

Paper punch

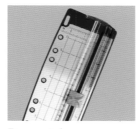

Paper trimmer

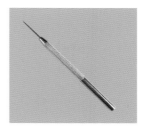

Piercing tool

Rubber stamps

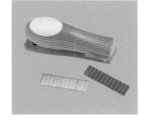

Stapler and colored staples

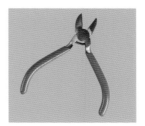

Wire cutter

Types of Boxes

Metal

Pocket-size candy and mint tins contain product information and advertising text that can be covered with paper, paints, and trims. New metal boxes are sold in scrapbooking and craft stores and are available without written material printed on them. They are available in square, round, rectangular, and heart shapes and come in white or silver. Some metal tins are sold with see-through lids as storage craft containers. Larger rounds with removable lids are sold as CD holders.

Paper

Paper, cardboard, and papier-mâché boxes come in round, square, heart, oblong, and novelty shapes such as sandals, books, and ring boxes.

Plastic

Mini-boxes made of plastic include mint dispensers and dental floss containers.

Wood

Small wooden boxes sold in craft stores are constructed with miniature hinges, handles, and clasps. Lids are made of solid wood, screen cloth, glass view windows, or carved or pressed textured panels.

Techniques

Adding glitter

For pinpoint accuracy, use a fine-point metal tip created especially for glue. The same tips can be used to apply a very fine, narrow line of glue. For thin smears of glitter, apply glue and spread around with fingertip or knife point. Glitter adheres best to wet, shiny glue within seconds of the glue being applied. Use a spoon to apply larger amounts of glitter and tap off excess.

Adhering fabric

Depending upon the thickness and sheerness of fabric or ribbon, several adhesives may be used. Fabric glue works on finer weaves, while drier acid-free adhesives work well on open weaves. Silk and rayon fabric and ribbon may show stains if very wet glues or anti-fray solutions are used. Test on a spare sample of the fabric. Double-sided tape works on most fabrics but may need special handling and tucking around curves and rounded sides.

Applying acrylic paint

Acrylic paints are used in a few projects and can usually be applied nicely with a foam brush. To make these projects in minutes, a quick wipe of paint and a light swipe afterward with a paper towel are usually all that is needed.

Applying alcohol ink

Available in small bottles with dropper tips, alcohol ink works only on shiny surfaces. Blending solution can be applied first to the blank surface to prolong the drying period and allow for more swirling and combining of the ink drops to produce stone-like finishes. Cosmetic sponges and makeup applicators can be used to produce different painted effects. Be sure to wear rubber gloves when using alcohol ink.

Applying sealer

Use on raw wood to seal before applying any other decoration. Use sealer on painted or papered wood, paper, metal, twigs, and stamps to give a final protective coat to a piece or to bring out the colors in an item. Artist's brushes, foam brushes, and paper towels can all be used to apply sealer.

Setting eyelets

To set an eyelet, punch a small hole in the paper where the eyelet is to be set. Insert eyelet through hole and position project face down on a craft mat. Using setting tool and hammer on a setting mat, flatten the eyelet's wrong side. *Note:* Some eyelet setters don't require a hammer; simply follow the manufacturer's instructions.

Prepping Boxes

Metal boxes

Miniature metal boxes sometimes carry unwanted printing and advertising. Hide wording or images with leafing pens or cover with decorative paper or fabric stickers. Alcohol ink will also cover most printed material on shiny surfaces with one or two coats. Primer and spray paint applied in thin coats can also provide a solid-color background.

Paper boxes

Boxes made from brown kraft paper or white cardboard or covered with decorative foil can be embellished with any number of items. A light wash of acrylic paint can evoke a timeworn look, or use more color for a brighter effect. Colored cardstock and sandpaper can be torn and layered, rubber stamped, or layered with ribbon.

Wood boxes

Raw wood boxes are ready to accept paper or fabric as is. For a nicer finish on wood handles or side strips, coat with clear sealer and then apply acrylic paint with a sponge brush. A simple once-over with sandpaper will refine the box even further. Similarly, spray stain provides an even finish of color or a more dramatic wood tone in just seconds.

CHAPTER 2

Good wishes celebrate the happy times and mend the little tears in the fabric of our days. Special mini-boxes can speak these thoughts for us even when the party is over or when we can't be there in person but are present in spirit. Best wishes are a pat on the back, a kiss for good luck. A little box can cheer on dreams or send a "Bon Voyage" message to a soon-to-be explorer. Celebrate promises kept and dreams fulfilled with a "Happy Anniversary" toast box. A happy occasion is sweetened with a "Congratulations" box filled with candies. And when the bumps in the road need smoothing over, a mini-box can give a sunny "Get Well" or "Cheer Up" hug.

Good Wishes Boxes

Celebration Cake

Materials

- Beads: small glass round, bugle, and micro beads in bright colors
- Boxes: 1½", 2" round tins with lids (1 each)
- Buttons: candle-shaped (11)
- Dimensional paint: white
- Glitter: clear micro-fine opalescent white
- Plastic knife and plate
- Strong-hold glue
- Toothpick

Instructions

1. With lids on boxes, center and glue smaller box on top of larger box.

2. Apply dimensional paint to both layers as if frosting a cake using plastic knife; allow to dry 30 minutes. *Note:* Use a disposable plate turned upside down as the base.

3. Place eight candles around second layer and three candles on top of "cake." Scatter beads and micro beads on top layer to look like candy sprinkles. Dust cake lightly with glitter.

4. When paint is stiff but still pliable, gently twist off bottom of large box. Make any repairs as needed with knife and toothpick. Push paint away from rims and clean edges. Allow paint to continue drying until completely hardened.

time-saving tip

Time to Dry

Depending on paint thickness and weather conditions, dimensional paint can take 6-24 hours to set completely. While the paint dries, use a kitchen knife or spatula periodically to loosen the bottom of the "cake" from the plate to prevent it from sticking.

Birthday Cards

Materials

- Acrylic paint: white
- Adhesives: craft glue, hot glue gun
- Box: kraft index card
- Circle punch reinforcement stickers
- Computer and printer
- Hole punch
- Pencil with eraser
- Ribbon: 1" (3 coordinating patterns)
- Scissors
- Silk flower
- Stickers: alphabet letters, epoxy dome

Instructions

1. Punch two holes in box lid, 1" from each end.

2. Cut two 12" pieces of 1" ribbon and insert through holes to form handle; tie knot at each end on inside of box.

3. Add reinforcement stickers randomly on front and back of file box. Wrap handful of stickers around corner edges.

4. Dip pencil eraser into acrylic paint and stamp on front, back, and sides of box. Reapply paint for each dot, removing excess before stamping. Stamp dots on fabric section; allow to dry. *Note:* Hold the box carefully to avoid smearing the dots.

5. Trim head of silk flower so back of flower lies flat. Glue flower head to snap closure using hot glue.

6. Using computer, print out word "wish" and adhere to epoxy dome sticker. Cut and knot 6" piece of ribbon. Glue ribbon and epoxy dome sticker onto center of flower. Attach alphabet stickers to front of box to spell "Happy Birthday."

time-saving tip

Embellishing with Circles

Binder hole reinforcement circles are available in various colors with a sticker backing. They are a quick way to enhance any project, especially a plain paper box with a larger, flat surface.

Bon Voyage

Materials

- Box: wooden mini-suitcase with handle
- Cardstock: cream
- Computer and printer
- Craft knife
- Decorative paper: teal textured plastic
- Double-sided tape
- Mini-brads: antique copper finish (3)
- Paper punch: tag shape (3 sizes)
- Piercing tool
- Ribbons: coordinating patterns (4)
- Scissors

Instructions

1. Cut rectangular piece of decorative paper to fit around front, back, and bottom of box; adhere with double-sided tape. *Note:* Paper should just touch but not cover the clasp hardware of the box.

2. Cut slit in paper on bottom of box around hinges using craft knife. Trim slit if needed for box to open and close freely.

3. Type phrases onto cardstock using computer. Punch into tag shapes; pierce hole at top. If desired, set eyelet at top. Thread ribbons through hole in tags and tie to suitcase handle.

4. Print "Bon Voyage" on cardstock and punch into tag shape; adhere to outside of suitcase using double-sided tape.

5. Punch two small, narrow tags out of teal paper and adhere, wrong sides together, with double-sided tape. Pierce bottom of tag twice and insert brads; pierce top of tags and insert third brad. Tie to handle with ribbon.

time-saving tip

Adapting the Theme

Bon voyage is not just for vacations; life changes bring moves to new places, too. Customize a suitcase for a friend transferring to a new job in a new city with travel-related embellishments. A Bon Voyage box is also perfect for a new college student when it is painted in school colors and embellished with images of a pizza, books, and a welcome mat.

28

Happy Anniversary

Materials

- Adhesives: acid-free dispenser, double-sided tape, glitter glue, hot glue gun
- Box: 5"x 3½" oval papier-mâché
- Computer and printer
- Corks in wire cages from champagne bottles (3)
- Decorative paper: subtle rose print, blue-and-white striped
- Glitter: ultra-fine clear opalescent
- Needle-nose pliers
- Paper punches: 1" heart punch; 3" oval scallop
- Ribbon: ¼" romantic-themed words; ½" blue silk
- Scissors: craft, small pinking shears
- Thin wooden disk: 2" diameter
- Wire cutters

Instructions

1. Cover top of box lid with rose decorative paper using acid-free adhesive. Print "Happy Anniversary to Us!" twice onto subtle rose decorative paper using computer; cut one into ¼" strip with small pinking shears and adhere inside bottom of box, halfway up side, using double-sided tape. Set aside second strip.

2. Cut 1⅜"-wide strip of blue striped paper; adhere with acid-free adhesive around outside of box (bottom piece). Adhere strip of blue silk ribbon with acid-free adhesive around center of blue striped paper. Layer romantic-themed ribbon on top of blue silk ribbon, adhering with acid-free adhesive.

3. **To create bistro chairs:** Holding U-shaped part of champagne wire cage in one hand, snip circular wire that connects all vertical wires at farthest point away from U-shaped part being held. Remove snipped piece of wire and set aside. (Remaining cage now resembles four-legged stool with one or two sharp feet.) Bend tips of "feet" into smoother shape using pliers. Attach reserved piece of wire, which should have an arched shape similar to upside-down "U," to stool piece by wrapping its wires around chair legs. Bend to adjust so chair sits level. Punch two hearts from rose paper and adhere to seats with double-sided tape.

4. **To create bistro table:** Snip cage same way as chair, except use only four-legged stool piece and discard rest of wire. Attach wooden disk to stool "seat" using hot glue gun. Smooth feet with pliers as necessary.

Champagne celebration

Drink the moment down

cheers!

Here's to another fine year!

Happ

Anniversary

to Us!

to cherish...to love honor & cherish...to love honor

Top: A miniature bistro set is secured on top of the box with a bit of hot glue.
Above: Sprinkle on clear glitter to disguise seams where materials meet.

Above: Scalloped ovals can be punched out of cardstock and joined together with a heart-shaped brad to create a mini-book of memories.

5. Attach bistro table and chairs to top of papered lid using dab of hot glue. Cut second "Happy Anniversary to Us!" into separate words. Adhere to box lid between table and chairs using acid-free adhesive. Adhere blue ribbon to outer band of lid with acid-free adhesive. Apply glitter glue to outer edge of lid top; sprinkle on glitter.

6. Print tiny phrases on computer and adhere to table and chairs with acid-free adhesive.

time-saving tip
Eliminating a Step
To speed up this project, cover the lid and box with paper and ribbon as described, but eliminate the bistro set. Wine labels can also be adhered onto the box and lid to add to the celebration.

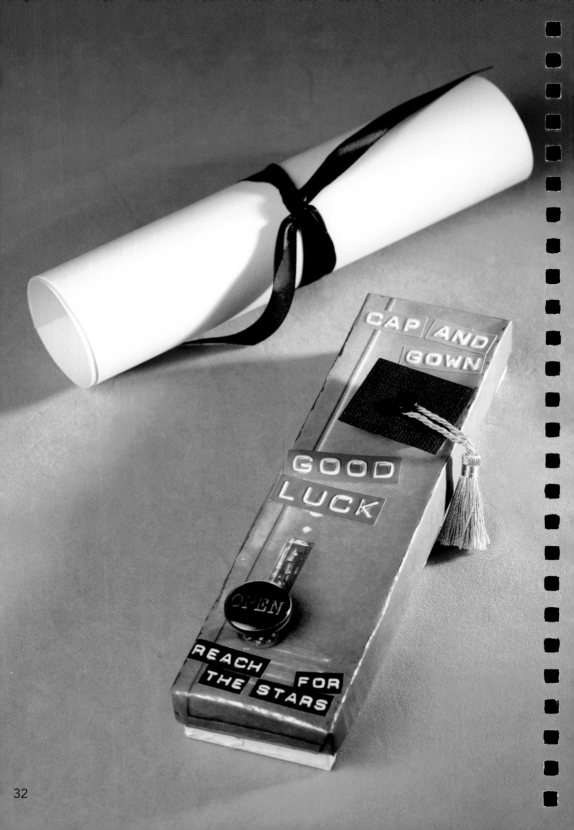

Congrats Graduate

Materials

- Adhesives: double-sided tape, foam dots, strong-hold glue
- Box: 2"x 7" cardboard
- Brad: black
- Cardstock: black
- Decorative knob
- Decorative paper: school-themed
- Handmade paper: off-white with metallic flakes
- Leafing pen: gold
- Piercing tool
- Scissors
- Stickers: inspirational messages
- Trim: gold satin tassel

Instructions

1. Cut decorative paper and cover exterior of box lid using double-sided tape.

2. Cut handmade paper and cover exterior of box bottom using double-sided tape. Highlight edges of box lid using gold leafing pen.

3. Cut 1½" square of black cardstock. Pierce center of cardstock and insert brad, opening prongs on back. Add foam dots onto back of cardstock square and attach to box lid.

4. Wrap gold tassel trim around brad to secure. Adhere stickers to box lid.

5. Adhere decorative knob to box lid using strong-hold glue. Adhere additional stickers around sides of box.

time-saving tip

Put in its Place

After the graduation festivities are over, use this keepsake box to save the prize of the day—the tassel. You'll always know where your memento is.

Congratulations

Materials

- Adhesives: craft glue, double-sided tape, vellum adhesive
- Box: 3" round tin
- Cardstock: white
- Computer and printer
- Decorative paper: green satin textured
- Eyelet setting tools
- Eyelets: large gold (2); dark pink (2)
- Iron

- Paper punches: decorative border; 2" tag
- Ribbons: ¼", 1½" green silk; 1½" pink, green, and yellow silk plaid; ¼" double-face satin, two-tone pink and gold
- Rub-ons: alphabet letters
- Scissors
- Tags: 1½" dark pink metal
- Vellum

Instructions

1. Cut 18" piece of two-tone pink and gold ribbon. Adhere around outer rim of tin lid using double-sided tape, allowing pink side of ribbon to show.

2. Adhere piece of double-sided tape to inside of tin lid. Tie one piece of wide plaid ribbon around lid with knot on center top. Press underside of lid to secure ribbon to tape already on the lid.

3. Adhere piece of double-sided tape to center of wide ribbon on inside of lid. Place wide green ribbon around uncovered part of lid and tie knot under and around first plaid ribbon.

time-saving tip

Ribbons Replace Paper

Use richly textured or unique ribbons instead of paper to "upholster" the outside of a tin box. A quick knot on top and a bit of tape underneath to secure it will transform a tin, paper, or wooden box into a festive party favor. Adapt the theme to a particular occasion by changing the wording on the tags.

Top: Consider ribbons that match a room's hue or the recipient's favorite colors.
Above: Add congratulatory messages with stickers, typed phrases, or rub-ons.

4. Tie plaid tails once more, this time around green knot. Press underside of lid to secure green ribbon to tape on plaid ribbon. Test lid to see that it fits easily. Loosen or tighten ribbons as necessary. Fan out the four tails and trim evenly. Add more tape inside lid if necessary to secure green ribbon.

5. Cut and adhere remaining 27" piece of wide green ribbon around side of box bottom using double-sided tape. *Note:* Ribbon should be narrow enough that a gap is kept clear of ribbon for the lid to rest. Trim and tuck ends under for a clean seam.

6. Adhere 18" piece of two-tone pink and gold ribbon, gold side out, around bottom edge of tin on top of green ribbon to form border. Line up seams and secure with double-sided tape. Repeat with gold ribbon around upper edge of green ribbon to form an upper border, matching seams in back.

7. **To create tags:** Cut vellum into 2½" tag. Trim bottom with border punch. Punch hole in top; layer pink and gold eyelets together, insert into tag hole, and set eyelets. Repeat steps with 2" green paper tag and pink and gold eyelets.

8. Type and print "congratulations"; adhere to vellum tag with vellum adhesive. Type and print "happy for you"; adhere to green tag with double-sided tape. Apply rub-ons to metal tag. Thread piece of ¼" green silk ribbon through hole in tags to make garland of greetings; knot ends. Tie top end of this ribbon to wide knotted bow and drape greeting tags to cascade down front of tin.

time-saving tip
Tags Made Easy

Tags are a versatile embellishment for mini-boxes. Tags can be purchased at office supply or craft stores. They also can be made using tag-shaped punches or die-cutting machines. Try color-coordinated cardstock, decorative papers and vellums, thin wood or cork, chipboard, plastic, linen, and metal. Add typed words, rub-ons, sticker alphabet letters, ribbon, bottle caps, eyelets, brads, new and old photos, or machine or hand stitching.

Get Well

Materials

- Adhesives: craft glue, double-sided tape
- Box: white bandage box with black handle
- Cardstock: off-white
- Computer and printer
- Decorative paper: red polka dot on pink background
- Embellishments: medical-themed
- Flower blossoms: red, white
- Paper punch: 2" heart
- Ribbons: coordinating patterns (4-5)
- Scissors

Instructions

1. Print "Get Well Kit" on off-white cardstock in red ink using computer; cut out using heart paper punch.

2. Cut two wings out of decorative paper; adhere behind heart using double-sided tape.

3. Adhere winged heart to front of box using double-sided tape.

4. Adhere embellishments and flower blossoms to front and back of box with craft glue.

5. Tie short strips of ribbons to handle and knot.

time-saving tip

Staying Healthy

Fill the Get Well box with strips of paper inscribed with inspirational quotes. The box also can be used to store packets of mosquito repellent, aloe vera, antihistamines, sunscreen, and ointment for cuts and scrapes.

Cheerfulness keeps up a kind of daylight in the mind, and fills it with a steady and perpetual serenity.

Joseph Addison

Cheer Up

Materials

- ⅛" hole punch
- Adhesives: craft glue, double-sided tape
- Box: 2" square kraft
- Brads: gold (2)
- Decorative paper: adhesive-backed leaf and sunflower blooms
- Eyelets: large sunflower-shaped (2); small gold (2)
- Hair elastic: tan
- Piercing tool
- Scissors
- Silk leaves: small
- Trim: ⅛" off-white braid
- Vellum sentiment

Instructions

1. Cut and adhere decorative paper to top and sides of box lid with double-sided tape. *Note:* Keep the lid off the box.

2. Glue braid trim around edges of lid to hide seams where papers meet.

3. Punch two holes on opposite sides of box using hole punch. *Note:* Holes should line up with each other and be centered on side of box when lid is on.

4. Insert gold brad into sunflower eyelet, then insert into small gold eyelet (acts as a spacer). Insert gold brad into hole in box and open prongs inside box. Repeat on other side.

5. Glue row of silk leaves around bottom of box.

6. Replace lid on box; close with elastic wrapped around sunflower eyelets. Slip vellum sentiment under elastic band.

time-saving tip

Gluing on Trims

Applying openwork braids and trims requires only a small amount of glue. A fine-tip applicator on a glue bottle allows more control. Avoid using double-sided tape on open trim as the exposed adhesive will catch unwanted dust or glitter.

CHAPTER 3

A mini-box dedicated to favorite things can be a gift in itself or a sweet tribute to passions and sentimental treasures. A summer day can be captured inside a decorated mini-sandal, while chocolate deserves a box because, well, it's chocolate. Favorite music for any occasion slips into a decorated gift tin, or bring nature indoors with a box inspired by bird watching. What was that great restaurant you discovered on a trip? Keep cards in a box dubbed "eats" for future reference or recommendations. Even that irresistible pet gets deserved recognition when honored on a special box that can be filled with tasty treats. Give a mini-box with a gift certificate or gift card and bestow an invitation to enjoy a few more favorite things.

A Summer Day

Materials

- Adhesives: craft glue, double-sided tape, glitter glue, glue stick
- Box: papier-mâché sandal
- Decorative paper: coordinating patterns (3)
- Flowers: 1" paper (3); 1¼" paper (1)
- Glitter: ultra-fine pale apricot
- Pencil
- Rhinestone: self-adhesive pink
- Ribbon: 2 coordinating patterns
- Scissors

Instructions

1. Trace outside of shoe onto decorative paper; cut out. Cut straight line about 1" in from edge at toe thong. Ease paper onto surface of box, trimming as needed to cover box. Adhere with glue stick. Repeat for side of lid and inside bottom of box.

2. Layer and adhere ribbon to side of bottom of box with double-sided tape.

3. Cover thong piece with paper and ribbon. Trim and tuck, then glue on paper flowers. Add rhinestone to flower center.

4. Cover outside bottom of box with second piece of decorative paper.

5. Apply glitter glue in very thin line on top of sandal where top and side papers meet; sprinkle on glitter. Repeat on inside of box, around edge where bottom and side wall meets; sprinkle on glitter.

time-saving tip

Shoe-Stopping Ideas

This charming summer sandal is perfect for sending a pool party invitation. It can also be used as a fun party favor. Just tuck in a little treat!

I LOVE CHOCOLATE

Chocolate Lover

Materials

- Adhesives: craft glue, double-sided tape, foam tape
- Beads (4)
- Box: 1½"x 2½" mint tin
- Cardstock: beige
- Computer and printer
- Decorative paper: brown floral embossed
- Pencil
- Sandpaper
- Scissors
- Trim: brown-and-white checkered; brown, green, and red rosette; brown beaded

Instructions

1. Lightly sand surface of tin. Draw outline of box on decorative paper. Cut four pieces, two for inside top and bottom and two for outside top and bottom. Glue onto tin.

2. Adhere checkered trim to bottom outer edge with double-sided tape.

3. Adhere rosette trim around edge of lid with double-sided tape.

4. Adhere beaded trim to outer edge of lid, closest to rimmed edge, with double-sided tape.

5. Glue beads to bottom of tin to serve as "feet."

6. Type small sentiment on cardstock and cut to 2"x ⅛". Cut points at each end like you would ribbon; attach diagonally to lid with small pieces of foam tape.

time-saving tip

Under Cover

Disguise the writing or embossing on an empty mint tin by covering the inside and outside with heavy decorative paper or cardstock. Test outside of lid for clearance by opening and closing a few times before gluing.

Bird Watching

Materials

- Acrylic paint: blue
- Adhesives: acid-free dispenser, craft glue, double-sided tape, glue dots
- Bird eggs: ½" long (3)
- Bird nest: 1½" diameter
- Box: 4" kraft
- Cardstock: beige, blue (to match acrylic paint)
- Craft wire: thin gold
- Foam brush
- Hole punch
- Inkpad: black
- Manila tags: 2"x 4" (6-8)
- Pencil: 3" bark-covered
- Raffia: natural-colored
- Rubber stamps: bird-themed, small alphabet letters
- Scissors: craft, scalloped-edge
- Skewer
- Spanish moss
- Twine

Instructions

1. Rubber stamp bird images onto blue paper. Tear edges close to image. With lid on box, determine even placement and adhere stamped papers to side of box using acid-free adhesive. Secure any loose ends with small amount of craft glue. Stamp one image directly onto inside bottom "floor" of box.

2. With lid off box, apply craft glue to side of lid band and layer several rows of raffia onto band. Press tightly for a good bond and reapply glue in spots as needed. *Note:* Leave a few loose, rough ends.

time-saving tip

Adapting the Theme

A nature-inspired theme can be achieved with nests, topiary trees, branches, and vines. The box is ideal to place on a writing desk, in a reading nook, or to nestle among a few gardening books on display.

Above: Trim shipping tags with scalloped-edge scissors or pinking shears and tie with twine to make a miniature bird watching log.

3. Wind 2-3 strands of gold wire in and around nest; snip wire into 4"-6" lengths. Curl 2-3 wire ends around skewer handle to form tendrils. Line with raffia bits and Spanish moss, securing in place with craft glue.

4. Paint eggs; allow to dry. Secure in place in nest with glue dots.

5. Adhere nest to lid with double-sided tape. Fill in a few areas, but not all, between nest and box lid with Spanish moss bits, securing in place with craft glue.

6. **To make bird watching log:** Cut office tags to fit inside box with scalloped-edge scissors, about 2" long. Rubber stamp top tag with words "Bird watching log"; hole punch top of tags. Cut 1' piece of twine and tie through tags;

Above: A rustic bark-covered pencil can be chiseled and finished at the top with twine to accompany the log.

knot ends of bow. Wrap piece of twine around top of pencil, securing in place with craft glue. Tuck inside box.

time-saving tip

Getting Book Smart

Little books can be made to fit into the smallest of mini-boxes. Punch squares, circles, or scalloped ovals and bind with brads, ribbon, twine, ball chain, metal binder clips, or bookbinding tape. A strip of 12" paper can be folded accordion style to form a booklet.

CD Gift

Materials

- Adhesives: acid-free dispenser, double-sided tape, foam dots, glue dots
- Box: CD tin
- Cardstock: chocolate brown, light pink, medium pink, sage green
- Craft knife
- Decorative paper: lime green with satin shimmer finish
- Die-cut machine
- Hole punch
- Paper cutter
- Paper punches: 1", 2½" daisy flower
- Pencil
- Rhinestones: self-adhesive lime green, shades of pink
- Ribbon: ¼" coordinating patterns (5)
- Rub-on letters
- Scissors
- Stapler
- Unusable CD

Instructions

1. Trace outside of lid onto brown cardstock; adhere to top of lid with double-sided tape.

2. **To add ribbon:** Cut three 4" strips of ribbon and staple to 7" strip of ribbon. Lay this long ribbon flat on tin to check placement. Adhere strip of ribbon to circles down right side, perpendicular to seam between two colors of paper using double-sided tape. Tuck ends of ribbon under circle and adhere circle to lid of tin.

time-saving tip

Making Music

Favorite custom play lists can be purchased and recorded for all occasions, including weddings, milestone birthday parties, and road trips. Personalize the CD by creating a thin sticker label available where blank discs are sold that coordinates with the CD Gift box.

Top: Mini-files can be hand cut and used as a title for the CD case or for a little message written inside the file. **Above:** Sparkling rhinestones attach to the center of daisies using glue dots or hot glue. Some are available with self-adhesive backs.

3. **To add flowers:** Punch large and small daisy shapes out of light and medium pink, sage green, and chocolate brown cardstock. Punch small daisies out of decorative paper; bend some petals up, away from surface of tin. Scatter large daisies on paper in vague triangle shape. Build rest of surface by layering smaller daisies in and around big flowers. Adhere large flowers with double-sided tape and smaller flowers with glue dots and foam dots. Adhere rhinestones to center of some of daisies.

Above: Cover an unusable disc with decorative paper to make a card for the inside of the tin.

4. Cut mini-file (rectangle folded in half with notch cut in top) from sage green cardstock. Apply rub-on letters to front side of file to spell out desired message. Embellish with ribbon or punches as desired.

5. Adhere file to tin with acid-free adhesive. If desired, write message in file.

6. **To make inside message:** Trace outside of tin onto both pink and brown cardstock. Cut ⅔ of circle from pink cardstock and one full circle of brown cardstock. Hole punch circle in center of pink cardstock. Paper punch 1" daisies at top then adhere pink piece on top of brown circle. Adhere to CD using double-sided tape.

time-saving tip

Alternate Use

For a different use, decorate the inside of the CD tin as a flat greeting card using thicker paper, such as cardstock, in addition to embellishments. Write your greeting on the paper-covered disc and place inside the decorated tin. Surprise the recipient by also tucking in cash or a gift card for purchasing tunes electronically, music equipment, or concert tickets.

Shell Collection

Materials

- Acrylic paint: white
- Adhesives: acid-free dispenser, craft glue, double-sided tape, foam dots, hot glue gun
- Box: 4" round kraft
- Decorative paper: beige, dark blue, light blue
- Foam brush
- Glitter: ultra-fine gold, light blue
- Inkpad: black
- Micro beads: beige, blue, green, light green
- Paper towel
- Rubber stamps: typewriter-style letters (2 sizes)
- Sandpaper: coarse grit
- Scissors
- Seashells
- Twill tape
- Twine

Instructions

1. Apply paint to rubber stamps with foam brush; remove excess with paper towel. Stamp "Sea" onto dark blue decorative paper; allow to dry. Cut into squares.

2. Tear strips of beige and dark and light blue decorative papers to mimic waves and roll edges. Adhere around outside of box bottom using acid-free adhesive. Tear sandpaper into irregular shapes and glue onto lid using double-sided tape.

time-saving tip

Painting Versus Inking

Using acrylic paint instead of ink when stamping can produce beautiful, variegated images. Cover foam stamps with paint, taking care to check for excessive paint and cleaning the stamp edges, then stamp.

Above: Rubber stamp a sentiment or title on a small office tag that can be trimmed to fit inside a box of seashells.

3. Adhere "Sea" letters to front outside of box using foam dots.

4. Stamp "by the" onto box to left of "Sea" using stamps and black inkpad.

5. Apply small amounts of craft glue to lower part of box, to right of "Sea," and onto lid at the 9 o'clock position. Sprinkle with beads, small shells, and both glitter colors.

Above: Craft glue is spread in a wave pattern and then covered with seed beads in ocean colors.

6. Attach two strips of twill tape to large shell using hot glue gun; adhere loose end to matching shell to form small book. (The twill hinge can be printed or plain.) Adhere shells to top of lid using hot glue gun.

7. Cut 20" piece of twine and tie around band of box lid. Knot in place, add dot of craft glue to secure, cut to trim, and unravel twine to look frayed.

8. If desired, adhere sandpaper, seashells, and tag inside box with hot glue gun.

time-saving tip

Making Sea & Sand

Sandy effects on boxes don't require loose sand and glue to achieve. Rather, tear strips of coarse-grit sandpaper to obtain a gently rolling edge. Tear paper toward you with your dominant hand, holding paper firmly with the other hand. Check for typing on reverse side so edges don't show print. Glue or tape in place and layer with cardstock in watery hues.

My grandmother's garden

Garden Gate

Materials

- Acrylic paint: off-white
- Adhesives: double-sided tape, strong-hold glue
- Box: 4" wooden box with hinged screen lid
- Charms: dragonfly, shovel
- Clay pots: ½" diameter (4)
- Colored pencils
- Foam brush
- Mini clothespin
- Paper towel
- Photograph: 1" square black-and-white garden-themed
- Picket fence
- Ribbon: pink velvet
- Scissors
- Stickers: flowers
- Trim: pink tassel

Instructions

1. Brush light coat of paint on fence and box, covering inside and outside only. *Note:* Leave the screen unpainted.

2. Remove excess paint by wiping with a paper towel, taking care that hinges are not painted; allow to dry 5 minutes. *Note:* A very light coat of paint on the clasp will not affect the mechanics of the box and actually adds to its character.

3. When dry, adhere fence to back of box lid with strong-hold glue; allow to dry. Glue pots to bottom of box to serve as "feet."

4. Adhere ribbon to top of box with double-sided tape. Adhere tassel trim to front of lid along top edge with seam in back. Apply flower stickers to box, ribbon, and fence. Adhere charms to top of box using strong-hold glue.

5. With colored pencils, color photograph's grass green, flowers pink and yellow, and clothing and skin as desired. Clip photo to fence with mini-clothespin.

time-saving tip

Adding Height

Mini-boxes can be elevated by all sorts of "feet." Try gluing on miniature flowerpots, glass or wooden beads, or game pieces.

I Love My Dog

Materials

- Adhesives: double-sided tape, glue stick
- Box: 3" round mint tin
- Cardstock: red
- Paper: textured white
- Pencil
- Photo of dog
- Ribbon: ¼", ⅜" decorative pet-themed ribbons
- Sandpaper
- Scissors: craft, decorative-edge
- Sticker: pet-themed

Instructions

1. Lightly sand surface of tin.

2. Trace tin lid and cut circle out of white textured paper; trace tin bottom on red cardstock then cut out. Trace tin bottom and with decorative-edge scissors, cut third circle out of red cardstock. Adhere white circle to lid and red circle to inside bottom of tin using double-sided tape. Adhere decorative-edge red circle to underside of tin.

3. Adhere sticker to white paper on lid. Adhere larger ribbon to outer rim of bottom of box with double-sided tape. Adhere narrower ribbon to outer rim of tin lid. *Note:* Be sure to match both seams at the back of the box.

4. Embellish sticker on lid with short strip of narrow ribbon.

5. **To make mini-book:** Fold 8"x 4" piece of red cardstock in half to make 4" square. Cut or punch 2½" circle partly on the fold to create round card. Add charm, if desired.

Favorite Restaurants

Materials

- Adhesives: double-sided tape, glue dots
- Box: 4" rectangular covered in red fabric
- Embellishments: 2" knife, fork, and spoon (2 each)
- Frame: 2" square
- Scissors
- Stickers: alphabet letters
- Trim: flower and leaf braid

Instructions

1. Cut and adhere trim to top of frame using double-sided tape.

2. Cut and adhere trim to sides of box lid using double-sided tape. If desired, repeat with additional row of ribbon on box bottom.

3. Adhere decorated frame to top of box to resemble a plate using double-sided tape.

4. Adhere silverware to box top, next to "plate", and around bottom of box using glue dots.

5. In opening of frame, adhere alphabet letters to spell "eats."

time-saving tip

Ready for Business

The Favorite Restaurants box is ideal for storing business cards from your favorite places. Whether they're local haunts or good eats discovered on a trip, you will enjoy sharing locales when friends ask for tips on good restaurants to try.

CHAPTER 4

Life's special memories arrive with the milestone moments marked by the engagement ring, the wedding cake, baby's arrival, and baby's first haircut. Ordinary, everyday moments can also bring their own special memories to savor: fun times with girlfriends, cheering a child's sports, and the adventure of a road trip or camping vacation. Celebrate a loved one or remember the good times with a mini-box that takes only minutes to make. Make a tiered cake for a special "extra" to give a bride or flower girl, or bring a bit of the "great outdoors" inside. Create a sports box to honor your athlete with customized team colors, uniform number, and team photo. No need to wait—the milestones and the everyday moments keep coming.

Special Memories Boxes

The Girls

Materials

- ⅛" hole punch
- Adhesives: double-sided tape, strong-hold glue
- Beads: ball-shaped (4)
- Box: 3" round tin
- Decorative paper: pink reptile embossed, pink diamond print
- Feather boa: pink
- Glass drawer knob with wing nut
- Hammer and nail
- Paper clips: swirl (8)
- Paper punches: 3", 1½" circle
- Pencil
- Rhinestones: self-adhesive clear (large, small)
- Rub-on letters
- Scissors
- Trim: ½" black textured plastic
- Upholstery tacks: flat head (4)

Instructions

1. Trace outer edge of bottom of box while rolling across pink reptile paper. (Shape will be somewhat curved.) Adhere to side of tin with double-sided tape at top and bottom of box side.

2. Cut circle out of pink reptile paper using 3" paper punch; adhere to lid with double-sided tape.

3. Hammer nail through center of lid. Remove nail and tap lid lightly with hammer to flatten hole.

4. Attach glass knob to lid, securing wing nut on underside of lid.

5. Wrap small piece of feather boa around knob; secure with double-sided tape. Glue large rhinestone to top of knob.

time-saving tip

Using Everyday Knobs

Drawer knobs today can easily pass for jewelry for the home. Consider these items to top off mini-boxes. Vintage styles, natural twig and insect shapes, and sports ball knobs can all be used to personalize boxes.

Top and above: Use a circle punch and round paper clips to link together pages for a mini-photo gallery of snapshots.

6. With lid on box, adhere black leather trim around side of lid using double-sided tape. Adhere row of rhinestones just below trim.

7. Dip upholstery tack in strong-hold glue and insert into ball-shaped bead. Squeeze small amount of same adhesive in four corners of underside of box. Attach flat head of tack-and-bead unit to glued spot. Repeat for remaining three corners. Allow to dry without moving box.

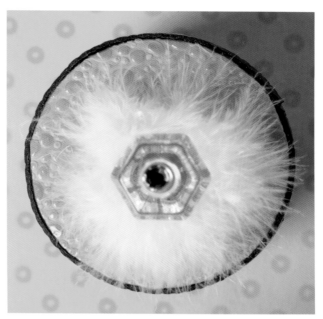

Above: A clear, self-adhesive rhinestone tops off the crystal drawer knob with a bit more glam.

8. **To make linked circles:** Using 1½" hole punch, create five circles out of pink diamond decorative paper. Punch two holes on opposite sides of circles; thread paper clips through holes, linking circles. Add rub-on letters to first circle.

time-saving tip

From Ordinary to Extraordinary

If you don't have a drawer knob on hand, consider stacking buttons on top of The Girls lid with strong-hold glue. The most humble gold plastic buttons can be embellished to look like a piece of fine vintage jewelry with a tasteful touch of glitter. Keep your eye out for simple treasures—you never know when a creative chord will be struck.

First Lock of Hair

Materials

- Adhesives: acid-free dispenser, double-sided tape

- Box: 3" round kraft

- Decorative paper: blue polka dots on white background

- Ribbon: 1¼" ivory double-faced satin

- Scissors: craft, fabric

- Stickers: bubble alphabet letters

- Trim: ¾" blue braid

Instructions

1. Cover side of box with decorative paper using acid-free adhesive. Cut large circle of decorative paper to cover lid, large enough to extend slightly over sides; adhere with acid-free adhesive.

2. Cut and adhere trim to rim of lid with double-sided tape. Apply bubble stickers to lid to spell out "My First Lock of Hair."

3. With lid off box, tie ribbon around box in a bow. Remove ribbon from box and hand pink edges with fabric scissors. Slip ribbon around box.

time-saving tip

Pinking Your Ribbon

Hand pinking with very sharp fabric scissors provides a luscious, custom look to double-faced satin ribbon. Experiment with deep cuts on inexpensive ribbon before you snip your final ribbon. For a quicker alternative, use pinking shears.

Child Sports

Materials

- Adhesives: craft glue, double-sided tape, foam dots
- Box: 2½"x 4" mint tin
- Chipboard number
- Computer and printer
- Decorative paper: patterned in team colors
- Embellishments: sports-themed
- Mesh net: self-adhesive
- Metal ribbon slide: jeweled circle
- Photo of athlete
- Scissors
- Stickers: sports-themed

Instructions

1. Cut and adhere rectangular piece of mesh net to top of lid to resemble volleyball net using craft glue for extra adhesion.

2. Cut and layer pieces of decorative paper in team colors using double-sided tape. Add photo of athlete using double-sided tape. Adhere chipboard number using foam dots then adhere sports-themed stickers.

3. Add ball sticker to center of ribbon slide; adhere to top of box with foam dot. Adhere remaining stickers and words printed using computer.

time-saving tip

Adapting a Theme

Sports magazines are a great source for sports-themed words and images. Clip photos of baseball stitching, golf clubs, or tennis balls to use for a particular sport. Round ball sports are nicely suited to attaching an image to a circular metal-rimmed office tag.

Camping Fun

Materials

- Adhesives: craft glue, double-sided tape, glue dots
- Box: mint tin
- Brads: round pewter (1); star-shaped (1)
- Canvas letters
- Craft knife
- Decorative paper: plaid
- Embellishments: outdoor-themed, words
- Fibers: green dyed raffia, natural twine
- Paper cutter
- Paper punch: large corner rounder
- Paper towel
- Scissors
- Sealer: clear acrylic satin finish
- Sticker: epoxy dome
- Twig: small
- Velvet leaf

Instructions

1. Cut three pieces of plaid paper and trim to fit both sides of lid; trim corners with corner rounder paper punch. *Note:* Leave the outside bottom of the tin uncovered.

2. Adhere velvet leaf to lower left corner with double-sided tape. Position some of leaf over edge of box lid.

3. Attach canvas CAMP letters to top of lid. *Note:* Letters "C" and "A" will partially cover the leaf.

4. Trim twig using craft knife so it lies flat. Wipe on acrylic sealer with paper towel; allow to dry 5 minutes.

5. Adhere narrow strip of double-sided tape across top of canvas letters; lay twig down on tape and trim ends to fit, if necessary.

6. Adhere embellishments using double-sided tape and add epoxy sticker.

7. Wrap narrow piece of double-sided tape around box bottom with two rows of green raffia. Tie row of twine on top of raffia and secure ends with dot of craft glue.

Wedding Wishes

Materials

- Adhesives: craft glue, double-sided tape
- Boxes: 1", 1½", and 2" round tins
- Dimensional paint: white
- Flowers: epoxy roses
- Leaves: epoxy, silver
- Paint tools: plastic knife and plate, star tip

Instructions

1. Stack boxes, from large to small, and adhere with double-sided tape. Remove lid of smallest box. Set aside for later use.

2. Using star tip, apply dimensional paint to bottom layer, around sides. *Note:* Avoid the seam between the lid and the box. Repeat for other two layers.

3. Apply paint stars to top of smallest box. *Note:* Paint will take 6-24 hours to dry, depending on weather conditions and paint thickness.

4. After 1 hour, while paint is still pliable, insert silver and epoxy leaves randomly around sides of cake layers.

5. Glue cluster of six epoxy roses onto top layer of cake. Glue seventh rose to center, on top of cluster; allow to dry. *Note:* Do not place lid on top of cake until all parts are dry. Remove excess paint to keep the seam between the lid and top layer clear.

time-saving tip

Boxes That Open

Only layers in which the seams are kept clear of dimensional paint will be functional as working boxes. To ensure your boxes open, keep dimensional paint from drying on seams.

Engagement

Materials

- Adhesives: craft glue with fine tip, glitter glue
- Box: shopping bag ring box
- Glitter: ultra-fine silver
- Paper flowers: small ivory (48)
- Scissors
- Trim: silver metallic braid

Instructions

1. Snip and remove string handles from shopping bag. Replace with metallic braid trim, knotting braid so handles stand upright.

2. Glue nine flowers to side of shopping bag. Glue nine more flowers on top of first layer, placing glue only in center of flowers with fine-tip applicator. Pull petals outward, on top flower, to lift away from backing. Repeat on other side of shopping bag.

3. Glue three flowers on each side of lid. Repeat with second layer of flowers, pulling petals away as before.

4. Apply tiny speck of glitter glue in center of each flower and immediately apply glitter; allow to dry.

time-saving tip

Pretty in Paper

Small paper flowers can be a real time saver. Start with a fabric- or paper-covered box in a nice color. Add a few flowers or pavé the entire surface so that a little of the background color shows through. Tiny rhinestones or glitter make ideal finishing touches.

New Baby

Materials

- Boxes: pink squares in graduated sizes (5)
- Craft glue with fine tip
- Fabric scissors
- Inkpad: black (optional)
- Rubber stamps: alphabet letters (optional)
- Tag: pink (optional)
- Trim: gold, pink gold metallic (5 coordinating patterns); narrow pink satin ribbon

Instructions

1. Apply narrow line of glue around outer edge of box lid; adhere smallest metallic trim. Repeat for each successive box, with larger metallic trim on larger boxes; allow to dry.

2. Stack boxes in tower shape and tie with pink satin ribbon.

3. *Optional:* Stamp desired sentiment on tag; tie to box.

time-saving tip

Easy Access

This sweet room decoration can be used to hold tiny keepsakes given to baby: a lace bonnet, crocheted booties, or a locket, as well as baby teeth or a lock of hair. Be sure to wrap delicates in acid-free archival tissue paper.

things for your trip:

on the road

HIGHWAYS
RD TRIP
AND BYWAYS

PLAY HERE Destination

Road Trip

Materials

- Adhesives: craft glue with fine tip, glitter glue, glue dots
- Box: 2½"x 4" mint tin with hinge opening
- Cardstock: rusty red
- Decorative paper: self-adhesive khaki linen
- Embellishments: metal travel-themed
- Glitter: ultra-fine black
- Leafing pens: copper, gold

- Mini brads: round silver (4)
- Paper cutter
- Paper punch: large corner rounder
- Pencil
- Ribbon: narrow black with white dotted line
- Scissors: craft, fabric
- Stickers: travel-themed
- Twine

Instructions

1. Paint sides of box and small amount of lid border with copper leafing pen to conceal printed material or undesired colors; allow to dry.

2. Trace lid and cut khaki fabric paper; trim with corner rounder as necessary. Peel backing and stick to lid.

3. Cut black ribbon to fit diagonally across tin lid. Attach with thin line of craft glue, wrapping edges under lid.

4. Embellish lid top with bits of torn map, phrases, or stickers. Attach brads to metal embellishment and attach to lid with glue dots.

5. Line lid with rusty red cardstock cut to fit; glue in place. Fill in any gaps around lid border with thin line of glitter glue then sprinkle on black glitter.

6. Glue twine around rim of lid. Adhere stickers so they can be seen from the side.

CHAPTER 5

Hopes and dreams for ourselves and others are captured in these exquisitely detailed, yet simple to make, mini-boxes. Recalling the life-size hope chests containing bridal gifts and family memorabilia, the "Hope Chest" can hold any number of things including hand-written dreams, photos related to a goal, or New Year's resolutions. The "Sweet Dreams" and "Joy" boxes are simple treasures sure to please all ages. The box-with-a-clock is a gentle reminder that it is "Time 2 Go For It," while the "Pointe Shoe" contains all the neces-saries for pointe shoe touch-ups and ballet dreams. Since autos were invented, they have been the focus of a car lover's dream. This versatile box can be used to store gas receipts or hold photos of a "Dream Car."

Hope Chest

Materials

- Adhesives: craft glue, double-sided tape
- Beads: flower and leaf (4); tube (4)
- Box: 4" wooden rectangle with hinged lid
- Charm: oval "Hope" (1)
- Ribbon: 1½" green velvet; ¼" variegated green
- Scissors
- Spray stain: green
- Trim: braid, floral

Instructions

1. Spray stain on box inside and out.

2. Adhere green velvet ribbon to top of box with double-sided tape. Adhere braid trim to bottom and to lid edges. Adhere floral trim next to braid trim.

3. Glue four tube beads to bottom of box to create "feet"; allow to dry.

4. Glue variegated green ribbon to lid top, around outer edge.

5. Glue four flower and leaf beads to top of box corners.

6. Glue "Hope" charm to center of lid top.

time-saving tip

Applying Spray Stain

When using spray stain, keep hinges and latches clear of excess paint. Spray stain adds color while allowing the wood grain to show through. Spray could render the hardware unusable.

Sweet Dreams

Materials

- Adhesives: craft glue, double-sided tape, glitter glue, strong-hold glue
- Beads: green wooden (4)
- Box: 2"x 2¼" mint tin
- Cardstock: green
- Decorative paper: green bamboo print, words
- Glitter: ultra-fine chartreuse
- Metal upholstery tacks (4)
- Ribbon: ¼" green silk
- Sandpaper
- Scissors: craft, decorative-edge

Instructions

1. Lightly sand exterior of tin.

2. Cut and glue bamboo print paper to top and bottom of box; trim to fit.

3. Cut and adhere word "Dreams" from decorative paper onto cardstock. Cut out with decorative-edge scissors to make 1" circle. Adhere to lid using double-sided tape.

4. Cut and adhere ribbon to sides of lid and bottom with double-sided tape.

5. To create "feet," slide bead onto upholstery tack and adhere together using strong-hold glue. Glue tack head to corner of underside of box; repeat to create four "feet."

6. Apply thin line of glitter glue where paper on lid meets ribbon on side. Sprinkle on glitter to hide seam.

time-saving tip

On a Personal Note

To personalize your mini-box, tuck in little messages printed or hand written on strips of paper. Sentiments could be love notes, inspirational words, favorite quotes, "honey do" tasks, or goals and wishes.

Joyful Times

Materials

- Adhesives: craft glue, double-sided tape, vellum tape
- Beads: ½" pink (4)
- Box: 2"-high tin
- Buttons: pink (4)
- Decorative paper: blue patterned
- Metal-rimmed tag: 1½" circle
- Micro beads: coral
- Paper word: "Joy"
- Ribbon: pink grosgrain
- Scissors
- Trim: thin coral polka dot; blue, pink rickrack
- Vellum: floral patterned

Instructions

1. Adhere ribbon around outside of box bottom with double-sided tape. Adhere polka dot trim on top of grosgrain ribbon.

2. Adhere grosgrain ribbon around lid with double-sided tape; layer with polka dot trim. Add second row of polka dot trim. Adhere blue rickrack on outer surface of top of lid; layer with pink rickrack on outer edge. *Note:* Pink rickrack will hang down slightly over the polka dot trim.

3. Outline word "Joy" with glue and cover with micro beads; allow to dry.

4. Cut and glue decorative paper onto metal-rimmed tag. Cut small flower from vellum and adhere to tag with vellum tape. Adhere rhinestone to center of vellum flower. Glue word "Joy" to tag. Adhere tag to box lid with double-sided tape.

5. Glue buttons to ends of all four beads; allow to dry. Glue buttons to underside of box for "feet."

time-saving tip

Customizing Tags

Metal-rimmed tags are readily available at office supply and scrapbook stores. Embellish them with brads, decorative paper, vellum, ribbon, charms, and words for a one-of-a-kind personalized look.

Time 2 Go For It

Materials

- Adhesives: craft glue, double-sided tape, glue dots
- Alphabet letters: fabric, metal, paper, epoxy, wood
- Battery-operated clockworks
- Box: large mint tin
- Charms: no. "2", flat alarm clock
- Decorative paper: self-adhesive distressed metallic gold, silver, and bronze
- Hammer and nail
- Inkpad: black
- Leafing pens: copper, gold
- Paper punch: large corner rounder
- Pencil
- Piercing tool
- Rubber stamp: woman's face

Instructions

1. Paint outer rim of box lid using gold and copper leafing pens. *Note:* This will disguise any gaps where the paper covers the writing on the tin.

2. Place clockworks inside box and partially close to see where works will need to protrude through lid. Mark inside of lid with pencil and then check that the spot will be somewhat centered on front.

3. Gently pierce metal lid using hammer and nail. Enlarge hole by spinning nail around, inside hole. Close lid and guide clockworks through hole. If it is a good fit, go to next step or enlarge hole as needed.

time-saving tip

Working with Adhesive Paper

Have extra sheets of the metallic sticker paper on hand for miscalculations. It is not repositionable and does not reapply well. If a mistake is made, start again with a new sheet. Once the stamped paper is in place, embellishing takes only a couple of minutes.

Above: Battery-operated clockworks fit snugly inside a large mint tin.

4. Cut pieces of scrap paper in same shape as box lid and rubber stamp with face; pierce hole in center of face to create a template. *Note:* Look for a spot in the center of the face, away from the nostrils and not in the eyes.

5. Stamp sheet of metallic paper with face stamp. Cut out rectangle for lid of tin, using template rectangle to guide placement of girl's face. Peel and stick paper with image to outside of box lid and pierce with tool through girl's image to clock hole. Cover bottom of box with metallic paper.

Above: For a collage look, mix and match clock hands or paint with leafing pens.

6. Assemble clock hands as instructed in clock package. Embellish face of clock by adhering alphabet letters to spell "Time" with glue dots. Adhere no. 2 charm at 2:00 with glue dot. Rubber stamp words "go for it" across bottom. Add clock charm at 9:00 with glue dot.

Getting the Right Fit

Battery-operated clockworks are sold at craft and hobby stores. Take your tin with you when purchasing the clockworks to ensure a good fit.

Inner Peace

Materials

- Adhesives: craft glue, glue dots
- Box: 4"-square white cardboard
- Decorative paper: 12"-square grass cloth
- Pencil
- Rub-on letters: white alphabet
- Scissors
- Stones (4)

Instructions

1. Trace grass cloth to fit on top of lid and inside of box. Trace all four sides of box lid on grass cloth; cut out all pieces and adhere in place with glue.

2. Adhere three stones to lid of box with glue dots. Add rub-on letters spelling "Peace" or "Love" to fourth rock and adhere inside box.

time-saving tip

Using Rub-On Letters

Rub-on letters adhere easily to a wide variety of surfaces. Paper, metal, glass, smooth wood, plastic, ribbon, twill trim, and even more unusual surfaces like stones, leaves, and silk flower petals will accept the letters.

Pointe Shoe

Materials

- Adhesives: double-sided tape, glue dots
- Box: 3¾" x 2¼" mint tin
- Cardstock: black
- Felted wool: coordinating colors (2)
- Metal alphabet letters
- Pencil
- Scissors: craft, pinking shears
- Small pointe shoe
- Trim: ribbon flower

Instructions

1. Trace bottom of tin on black cardstock; cut two pieces this size.

2. Adhere one piece of cardstock to underside of tin using double-sided tape. Adhere second piece to inside bottom of tin. Repeat procedure for outside and inside top of tin.

3. Adhere trim to outside perimeter of top and bottom of tin using double-sided tape.

4. Cut piece of felted wool ¼" smaller than top of tin using pinking shears. Cut piece of felted wool ¼" smaller than bottom of box. Adhere wool pieces to top of lid and underside of box with double-sided tape.

5. Cut strip of coordinating wool with pinking shears; adhere to top of lid. Spell out "pointe" with alphabet letters; adhere to felt using double-sided tape.

6. Attach small pointe shoe to top of box using glue dots.

time-saving tip

Staying Put

When creating a box that will hold small metal objects such as sewing pins and needles, glue a small magnet to the inside of the lid. The magnet will keep items from falling out of the box when opened.

Dream Car

Materials

- Adhesives: acid-free dispenser, double-sided tape, glue dots
- Box: round mint tin
- Brads: mini gold (2); silver with screw head (1)
- Charms: car-themed (1); magnetic wheels (4); steering wheel (1)
- Decorative paper: gold metallic; gray diamond steel pattern
- Paper punches: ½", 2" circles
- Photo: black-and-white of dream car
- Sticker: epoxy dome with word "Dream"
- Tags: alphabet letters
- Trim: black-and-white checkerboard

Instructions

1. Punch 2" circle out of gold metallic paper. Punch out half a circle with ½" hole punch (to make notch). Adhere to lid with double-sided tape.

2. Adhere steering wheel charm on left side of lid with rolled-up glue dots. Adhere dream sticker on right side.

3. Insert mini gold brads in letters "C" and "A" and screw head brad in letter "R"; open prongs to flatten. Adhere to top of tin using glue dots. Adhere photo to upper left of tin with glue dot.

4. Punch 2" circle out of diamond steel paper. Adhere to outside bottom of tin using acid-free adhesive. Adhere trim to outside edge of tin bottom using double-sided tape. Stick magnetic wheels on bottom of box or secure with glue dots.

5. Bend remaining car-themed charm and adhere to outer edge of tin lid with glue dots.

time-saving tip

Clever Embellishments

When using round mint boxes with a "press" mechanism, be sure the press button is not covered. Punch a ½" circle "scoop" notch to reveal the press button, then highlight it with a clever embellishment.

Love Always

Materials

- Adhesives: craft glue, double-sided tape, glue dots
- Box: 3½" heart-shaped wood with hinged lift–up lid
- Cardstock: red
- Ornament: carved ivory heart
- Paper towel
- Pencil
- Ribbon: ¼" coordinating patterned; ⅜" solid red
- Scissors: craft, decorative-edge
- Sealer: satin glaze
- Sentiment (optional)
- Spray stain: rusty red
- Trim: gold braid

Instructions

1. Spray box inside and out with stain, following manufacturer's instructions. Wipe excess stain from clasp or hardware; allow to dry. *Note:* Keep area where lid and box meet free from pools of stain liquid.

2. Lightly glaze heart ornament with clear sealer; set aside to dry.

3. Measure around heart lid and base with red ribbon and add ½" for folding under at seams. Cut and adhere with double-sided tape with seam at back. Trim ends and turn under; secure with double-sided tape.

4. Layer strip of coordinating patterned ribbon over red ribbon. Cut another strip of same patterned ribbon to fit around side band of heart lid and adhere with double-sided tape. Cover seam at back with gold trim and cut to fit; seal ends with glue.

5. Cut red cardstock in heart shape to follow the outline of heart ornament plus ½" border using decorative-edge scissors. Glue paper to top of lid; adhere heart ornament to center of paper using glue dots. If desired, decorate inside of box with paper heart and sentiment.

CHAPTER 6

Some details in modern life—house keys, credit cards, business cards, postage stamps, and cell phones—could use some organizing. Practical Purposes boxes can be embellished to hold spare keys for houseguests or a helpful neighbor, while excess credit cards can be cleared from wallets and stowed stylishly. Make a snappy business card case in minutes or keep spare change close by for laundry tasks. With little effort, you can have mending supplies at hand for inevitable repairs. A mint tin becomes a sewing kit pretty enough to grace a dresser top, while a broken cell phone can take on a glittering new life as a unique miniature address book box with foldout pages.

Practical Purposes Boxes

House Key

Materials

- Adhesives: craft glue, double-sided tape
- Box: 3¾" x 2¼" mint tin
- Charms: antique keys (2)
- Decorative paper: handmade with metallic flecks
- Ribbon (optional)
- Stickers: alphabet letters

Instructions

1. Carefully hold box over heat source to melt metal, about 5-10 minutes on each side, to age its surface.

2. Tear decorative paper so rough edges fit within corners of top of lid. Adhere to top of box with double-sided tape.

3. Attach sticker letters to top left corner to spell "house."

4. Glue antique key to top of lid.

5. Line interior of box bottom with piece of torn handmade paper; glue in place.

6. Glue second antique key to inside of lid. If desired, tie ribbon to house key and place inside for safekeeping.

time-saving tip

Make it Easy

Houseguests will appreciate having their own key while visiting your home. This key box can also be given to the neighbor who holds your spare key.

Credit Card Holder

Materials

- Adhesives: craft glue, double-sided tape, glue dots
- Box: 2½"x 3¾" mint tin
- Cardstock: beige
- Charms: metallic book plate (1), dollar sign (3)
- Computer and printer
- Cosmetic sponge
- Decorative paper: green textured plastic
- Leafing pens: copper, gold
- Mini brads: gold (2)
- Paper punch: large corner rounder
- Scissors

Instructions

1. Paint charms, bookplate, and brads with copper and gold leafing pens. Wipe and smudge with cosmetic sponge to mix colors; allow to dry.

2. Paint edges of tin with copper pen, accenting with touches of gold pen. Wipe and smudge; allow to dry.

3. Cut four pieces of decorative paper to fit box lid and bottom of box; round corners with punch. Adhere to lid outside, inside, bottom inside, and bottom outside using double-sided tape. *Note:* Use craft glue to secure edges of decorative paper.

4. Add dollar sign charms to upper left corner of lid with glue dots. Insert brads into holes on bookplate; open prongs on back to secure. *Note:* If necessary, trim brads so prongs cannot be seen.

5. Type and print "Credit Cards" on cardstock; insert in bookplate. Adhere bookplate to front of lid using rolled-up glue dots.

time-saving tip

Handy to Have

The Credit Card Holder can serve as a catchall for extra cards, duplicates, or seldom-used accounts. Tuck them in your desk or dresser for easy access.

Stamps Storage

Materials

- Acrylic paint: white
- Adhesives: acid-free dispenser, craft glue, foam tape
- Box: 1½" square kraft paper
- Foam brush
- Frames: white pressed metal with scalloped border (2)
- Paper towel
- Ribbon: ½" blue grosgrain
- Scissors
- Sealers: clear acrylic, satin finish
- Stamps: shades of blue

Instructions

1. Brush on thin coat of white paint inside and outside of box and lid. Use paper towel to wipe off excess and create distressed look.

2. Cut small pieces of ribbon, about 1" long. Glue to all four side panels of lid. Match up ribbons for straight lines. *Note:* Bulky rolled seams are unnecessary on the small pieces; gluing should be sufficient with this kind of ribbon.

3. Attach box base to frame using foam tape (frame should be right-side up, centered with paper box). Attach foam tape to center of wrong side of remaining frame. Place frame, foam side down, on lid of paper box.

4. Adhere stamps to top and interior of box using acid-free adhesive. Secure any loose corners with craft glue. If desired, apply thin coat of acrylic sealer to top of all stamps with paper towel; wipe off excess.

Business Card Holder

Materials

- Adhesive-backed trim: black
- Adhesives: craft glue, foam dots
- Box: slender breath mint tin
- Cardstock tag: beige
- Decorative paper: self-adhesive fabric
- Pencil
- Scissors: craft, fabric
- Small charm
- Stickers: alphabet letters

Instructions

1. Trace container lid and bottom on backside of self-adhesive fabric. Cut two pieces to fit lid and bottom of box.

2. Cover outside bottom of box and lid with self-adhesive fabric. Adhere trim onto outside edges of lid.

3. Spell out "I Mean Business" with alphabet stickers; add to tag. Glue charm onto tag.

4. Attach tag to top of lid with foam dots.

time-saving tip

We're in Business

Save time searching for numbers by making a business card holder to store business cards of your favorite home decorating, repair vendors, and service people. Painters, carpenters, and window covering business cards can be convenient to have on hand when you or your friends are moving or remodeling.

Laundry Money

Materials

- Adhesives: double-sided tape, glitter glue
- Box: 2½" x 3¾" tin with hinged lid
- Decorative paper: self-adhesive fabric
- Foam packing material
- Glitter: ultra-fine, large flakes clear opalescent
- Paper cup, plastic spoon
- Permanent inkpad: black
- Rubber stamps: alphabet letters, money symbol
- Scissors: craft, fabric
- Stickers: self-adhesive circle epoxy domes, small and medium

Instructions

1. Cut and adhere self-adhesive fabric paper to top of tin lid.

2. Cut and adhere narrow strip of fabric paper onto sides of lid.

3. **To create bubbles:** Crumble foam into paper cup. Coat with glitter glue. Stir with plastic spoon, breaking up big chunks. Place wet pieces around edges of lid. Using fingers and spoon, arrange to achieve effect of soap bubbles. Sprinkle with both sizes of glitter. While drying, sprinkle large flake opalescent glitter on sticky side of circle domes.

4. When "bubbles" are completely dry, glue to top of box. Tuck domes under and around bubbles to look like water drops.

5. Rubber stamp "laundry money" and "$$$" on lid. If desired, rubber stamp "dormitory = dirty room" onto fabric paper and adhere on inside of lid with double-sided tape.

time-saving tip

Easy Stamping Fix

If mistakes are made while rubber stamping, just stamp sentiment or symbols onto a scrap of fabric paper and attach it on top of the mistake for a layered look.

Sewing Kit

Materials

- Adhesives: acid-free dispenser, double-sided tape, glue dots, strong-hold glue
- Box: 2½" x 3¾" mint tin
- Button: ¼" white
- Cardstock: blue, cream
- Charms: metal alphabet letters
- Decorative paper: measuring tape
- Fabric: self-adhesive blue-and-green prints
- Paper punch: large corner rounder
- Pencil
- Ribbon: ⅜" black-and-white gingham
- Scissors: craft, fabric
- Sewing kit supplies
- Snap: small
- Thimbles: flat-topped steel (4)
- Tissue sewing pattern

Instructions

1. Trace bottom of tin onto blue cardstock and cut out. Punch each corner with corner rounder. Repeat for inside bottom of tin. Adhere cardstock with double-sided tape. Trace tin lid onto blue cardstock and cut out. Adhere to interior only of box with acid-free adhesive.

2. Trim piece of fabric to 1¾" square, punching upper left corner with corner rounder. Peel and stick to upper left corner of tin lid. Repeat for upper right corner. Cut third square and trim to fit center between the two fabric corners.

3. Trim second piece of fabric to 1¾" x 3¾", punching lower left corner with corner rounder. Trim right side to line up with square sticker above it and then punch lower right corner with corner rounder. Peel and stick to lid. *Note:* Pieces can be overlapped for a patchwork effect. The seam between the squares and rectangle will be covered by embellishments.

time-saving tip

Stash or Carry

For quick fixes, a sewing kit can be tucked in your purse, kept in a desk drawer at the office, stashed in the glove compartment of a car, or left in a suitcase.

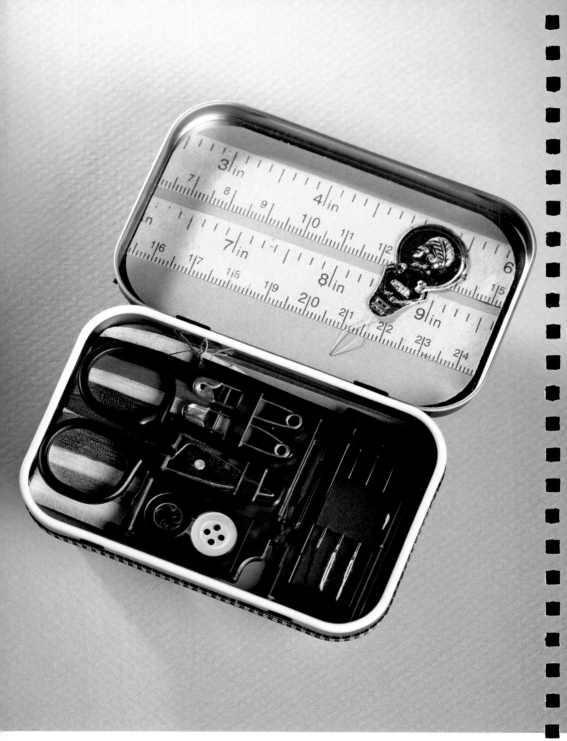

Above: A sewing kit is complete with small scissors, a needle threader, and spare buttons.

4. Adhere tissue pattern to cream cardstock using acid-free adhesive; cut piece 1" wide. Adhere on top of lid horizontally, covering seam between row of fabric squares and fabric rectangle. Trim ends.

5. Cut strip of measuring tape paper to fit lid vertically; adhere on left side of box.

Above: Cut, peel, and stick on adhesive fabrics for an easy way to decorate a mint tin lid.

6. Cut 4" strip of ribbon and tie in knot. Trim tails to 1" and adhere to top of button with glue dots. Adhere button embellishment to upper left side of lid on measuring tape using glue dot.

7. Adhere snap to lower right side of lid with glue dot. Adhere "SEW" letters to lid.

8. Adhere ribbon around outer rim of box bottom using double-sided tape.

9. Adhere thimbles to bottom of tin for "feet" using strong-hold glue; allow to dry.

10. Fill sewing kit with supplies as desired.

time-saving tip

Quick Coverup

Keep an eye out for fabric stickers that strike your fancy. They can be cut to fit for quick, easy coverage of a tin or other mini-box. Punched or die-cut fabric stickers also make unique embellishments.

Sewing Pins

Materials

- Adhesives: double-sided tape, glitter glue
- Alcohol ink: butterscotch, magenta, silver metallic
- Alcohol ink blending solution
- Box: rectangular mint tin with side opening and hinged lid
- Button: gold epoxy square flower
- Eye shadow applicators (3)
- Glitter: ultra-fine gold, green
- Newspaper
- Rubber gloves

Instructions

1. Sprinkle several dots of magenta alcohol ink on outside of box front (lid should be closed). Shake and rotate box and tap on newspaper to obtain swirls and patterns. Quickly add drops of the other two colors to center of magenta areas. Tap, rotate, and shake to obtain patterns, using eye shadow applicator to blend and blending solution when surface becomes too dry. *Note:* Be sure to wear rubber gloves when using alcohol ink.

2. Reapply inks as necessary until desired effect is achieved. Repeat process on sides, back, and lid. *Note:* Be careful not to let ink get under the lid. Wipe dry the underside of the lid as necessary.

3. Repeat process on button. When dry, place dots of glitter glue in center of flowers on button and sprinkle with gold and green glitter.

4. Attach back of button to front of box with double-sided tape.

time-saving tip

Giving Buttons a Makeover

There's no need to search out interesting buttons. Alcohol ink dries immediately and can be used to enhance the most unlikely bits of filigree. Inexpensive buttons are available at craft stores by the pound.

Phone Book

Materials

- Adhesives: craft glue, double-sided tape, glitter glue
- Box: 2" x 2¼" mint tin
- Cell phone face
- Glitter: ultra-fine gold, silver
- Handmade paper: black with metallic flecks, gold mulberry (optional)
- Leafing pens: gold, silver
- Scissors

Instructions

1. Apply glitter glue and sprinkle silver glitter on silver parts of phone face. Repeat with gold glitter for gold parts; allow to dry.

2. Trim phone face to fit mint tin and adhere using double-sided tape. *Note:* Cover any text on the tin with torn handmade paper using craft glue.

3. If desired, fold paper to create address book; tuck inside box.

time-saving tip

Alternate Box Idea

Rather than a mint tin, consider using a small papier-mâché book. Adhere metallic paper to the exterior of the box, gold leaf the "page edges," add bubble letters down the spine of the book to spell out "Addresses," and then top off with the glittered cell phone face.

METRIC EQUIVALENCY CHARTS

inches to millimeters and centimeters
(mm-millimeters, cm-centimeters)

inches	mm	cm	inches	cm	inches	cm
1/8	3	0.3	9	22.9	30	76.2
1/4	6	0.6	10	25.4	31	78.7
1/2	13	1.3	12	30.5	33	83.8
5/8	16	1.6	13	33.0	34	86.4
3/4	19	1.9	14	35.6	35	88.9
7/8	22	2.2	15	38.1	36	91.4
1	25	2.5	16	40.6	37	94.0
1 1/4	32	3.2	17	43.2	38	96.5
1 1/2	38	3.8	18	45.7	39	99.1
1 3/4	44	4.4	19	48.3	40	101.6
2	51	5.1	20	50.8	41	104.1
2 1/2	64	6.4	21	53.3	42	106.7
3	76	7.6	22	55.9	43	109.2
3 1/2	89	8.9	23	58.4	44	111.8
4	102	10.2	24	61.0	45	114.3
4 1/2	114	11.4	25	63.5	46	116.8
5	127	12.7	26	66.0	47	119.4
6	152	15.2	27	68.6	48	121.9
7	178	17.8	28	71.1	49	124.5
8	203	20.3	29	73.7	50	127.0

yards to meters

yards	meters	yards	meters	yards	meters	yards	meters	yards	meters
1/8	0.11	2 1/8	1.94	4 1/8	3.77	6 1/8	5.60	8 1/8	7.43
1/4	0.23	2 1/4	2.06	4 1/4	3.89	6 1/4	5.72	8 1/4	7.54
3/8	0.34	2 3/8	2.17	4 3/8	4.00	6 3/8	5.83	8 3/8	7.66
1/2	0.46	2 1/2	2.29	4 1/2	4.11	6 1/2	5.94	8 1/2	7.77
5/8	0.57	2 5/8	2.40	4 5/8	4.23	6 5/8	6.06	8 5/8	7.89
3/4	0.69	2 3/4	2.51	4 3/4	4.34	6 3/4	6.17	8 3/4	8.00
7/8	0.80	2 7/8	2.63	4 7/8	4.46	6 7/8	6.29	8 7/8	8.12
1	0.91	3	2.74	5	4.57	7	6.40	9	8.23
1 1/8	1.03	3 1/8	2.86	5 1/8	4.69	7 1/8	6.52	9 1/8	8.34
1 1/4	1.14	3 1/4	2.97	5 1/4	4.80	7 1/4	6.63	9 1/4	8.46
1 3/8	1.26	3 3/8	3.09	5 3/8	4.91	7 3/8	6.74	9 3/8	8.57
1 1/2	1.37	3 1/2	3.20	5 1/2	5.03	7 1/2	6.86	9 1/2	8.69
1 5/8	1.49	3 5/8	3.31	5 5/8	5.14	7 5/8	6.97	9 5/8	8.80
1 3/4	1.60	3 3/4	3.43	5 3/4	5.26	7 3/4	7.09	9 3/4	8.92
1 7/8	1.71	3 7/8	3.54	5 7/8	5.37	7 7/8	7.20	9 7/8	9.03
2	1.83	4	3.66	6	5.49	8	7.32	10	9.14

INDEX